Nita M

Breakfast
Cookbook

Nita Mehta

B.Sc. (Home Science), M.Sc. (Food and Nutrition), Gold Medalist

Nita Mehta's

Breakfast
Cookbook

ISBN   978-81-7869-186-2

Exclusive Distributor:

DIVISION OF: INFORMATION SCIENCE INDUSTRIES (CANADA) LIMITED

1169 Parisien St., Ottawa, Ont., K1B 4W4,
Tel: 613.745.3098 Fax: 613.745.7533
e-mail: amproductions@rogers.com
web: www.amproductions.ca

Published by:

SNAB
Publishers Pvt. Ltd.
3A/3 Asaf Ali Road,
New Delhi - 110002
Tel: 23252948, 23250091
Telefax:91-11-23250091
INDIA

Editorial and Marketing office:
E-159, Greater Kailash-II, N.Delhi-48
Fax: 91-11-29225218, 29229558
Tel: 91-11-29214011, 29218727, 29218574
E-Mail: nitamehta@email.com, nitamehta@nitamehta.com
*Website:*http://www.nitamehta.com
Website: http://www.snabindia.com

Printed at:

PRESSTECH LITHO PVT. LTD.,GREATER NOIDA

Price: $ 5.95

Contents

Omelettes & Egg Recipes 6

Freshly Baked Breads & Grilled Bites 15

Croquettes & Sausages 27

Pancakes & Other Recipes 35

Glossary 48

Introduction

A healthy breakfast makes the day go better. Breakfast, the first meal of the day, should be well balanced, nutritive and sustaining. It should have complex carbohydrates from cereals such as bread, cornflakes, oats, buns etc. and good quality proteins from eggs, meat, cheese and milk. Fruits and fresh vegetables give you a supply of vitamins and minerals.

This book has a collection of tempting recipes – hearty, wholesome omelettes and pancakes, freshly baked breads flavoured with herbs for the family, as well as elegant and attractive croquettes and sausage recipes for a more formal breakfast. Breakfast foods are comforting and cosy – many hotels recognise this and serve breakfast to homesick travellers throughout the day and night!

All the recipes are quick and easy to prepare, keeping in mind the shortage of time at that hour of the morning. No special ingredients are required – all of them are likely to be in your kitchen already. So, get set to give Breakfast a special place in meal planning in your home.

Nita Mehta

INTERNATIONAL CONVERSION GUIDE

These are not exact equivalents; they've been rounded-off to make measuring easier.

WEIGHTS & MEASURES

METRIC	IMPERIAL
15 g	½ oz
30 g	1 oz
60 g	2 oz
90 g	3 oz
125 g	4 oz (¼ lb)
155 g	5 oz
185 g	6 oz
220 g	7 oz
250 g	8 oz (½ lb)
280 g	9 oz
315 g	10 oz
345 g	11 oz
375 g	12 oz (¾ lb)
410 g	13 oz
440 g	14 oz
470 g	15 oz
500 g	16 oz (1 lb)
750 g	24 oz (1½ lb)
1 kg	30 oz (2 lb)

LIQUID MEASURES

METRIC	IMPERIAL
30 ml	1 fluid oz
60 ml	2 fluid oz
100 ml	3 fluid oz
125 ml	4 fluid oz
150 ml	5 fluid oz (¼ pint/1 gill)
190 ml	6 fluid oz
250 ml	8 fluid oz
300 ml	10 fluid oz (½ pint)
500 ml	16 fluid oz
600 ml	20 fluid oz (1 pint)
1000 ml	1¾ pints

CUPS & SPOON MEASURES

METRIC	IMPERIAL
1 ml	¼ tsp
2 ml	½ tsp
5 ml	1 tsp
15 ml	1 tbsp
60 ml	¼ cup
125 ml	½ cup
250 ml	1 cup

HELPFUL MEASURES

METRIC	IMPERIAL
3 mm	1/8 in
6 mm	¼ in
1 cm	½ in
2 cm	¾ in
2.5 cm	1 in
5 cm	2 in
6 cm	2½ in
8 cm	3 in
10 cm	4 in
13 cm	5 in
15 cm	6 in
18 cm	7 in
20 cm	8 in
23 cm	9 in
25 cm	10 in
28 cm	11 in
30 cm	12 in (1ft)

HOW TO MEASURE

When using the graduated metric measuring cups, it is important to shake the dry ingredients loosely into the required cup. Do not tap the cup on the table, or pack the ingredients into the cup unless otherwise directed. Level top of cup with a knife. When using graduated metric measuring spoons, level top of spoon with a knife. When measuring liquids in the jug, place jug on a flat surface, check for accuracy at eye level.

OVEN TEMPERATURE

These oven temperatures are only a guide. Always check the manufacturer's manual.

	°C (Celsius)	°F (Fahrenheit)	Gas Mark
Very low	120	250	1
Low	150	300	2
Moderately low	160	325	3
Moderate	180	350	4
Moderately high	190	375	5
High	200	400	6
Very high	230	450	7

Omelettes
& Egg Recipes

Spanish Omelette

A hearty omelette filled with vegetables and cheese – follow these steps and cook it to perfection.

Serves 2 (Makes 1 thick omelette)

INGREDIENTS

4 eggs
2 tbsp milk
½ tsp salt, ½ tsp pepper
¼ cup chopped green bell peppers or green onions
½ tomato - chopped
3-4 mushrooms - finely sliced
2 slices ham - finely chopped
or
½ cup boiled and shredded chicken
¼ cup grated cheddar cheese
1 tbsp butter or oil

METHOD

1 Beat the eggs with salt, pepper & milk till fluffy.

2 Heat butter or oil in an 8" diameter nonstick skillet/pan, keeping the heat low. Pour the eggs and roll the pan. Lift edges of the omelette and tilt the pan gently to let the liquid egg roll under.

3 Sprinkle green peppers, tomato, mushrooms and ham on top and press gently. Sprinkle a pinch of salt.

4 Sprinkle cheese and cover the pan. Cook for 2 minutes on low heat till the vegetables get steamed and the cheese melts.

5 Serve with vegetable side up. Cut into wedges. Serve hot with bread.

Nutty Egg Spread in Panini

Everybody's favourite ingredients make a Number One spread using cheese, butter, raisins and nuts mixed with hard-boiled eggs.

Serves 2

INGREDIENTS

2 panini breads - split into halves horizontally or 4 slices thickly sliced bread
2 eggs - hard-boiled
1½ tbsp salted butter
4 tbsp grated cheddar cheese
1 tbsp raisins (*kishmish*)
¼ tsp pepper
¼ tsp salt, to taste
1 tbsp finely chopped celery
1 tbsp slivered almonds or any other chopped nuts
4 tbsp milk, approx.

METHOD

1. Cut panini into 2 piece horizontally. Pan toast in a skillet or a non stick pan till crisp.

2. Grate and mash the boiled eggs. Add all ingredients, adding enough milk to get a good paste of spreading consistency. Check salt and add if needed.

3. Spread a thick layer of egg spread on the bottom piece of bread. Cover with the top piece. Serve.

Chicken Omelette

Chicken is microwaved for quick cooking then mixed with tomatoes and sprinkled over the omelette – this one is for any time of the day, not just breakfast!

Makes 1

INGREDIENTS

2 eggs
(125 g/4 oz) chicken, 1 tsp oil
1 small tomato - cut into 4, deseeded and chopped without pulp
1 green onion - chopped finely along with the greens
½ tsp salt & ¼ tsp pepper, or to taste
1 tbsp butter

METHOD

1. Place the chicken with 1 tsp oil and ¼ tsp salt in a small microproof bowl. Mix. Cover with a plastic wrap and microwave for 3 minutes. Cool. Debone chicken, cut into small pieces. Mix chicken with tomatoes. Keep aside.

2. Beat eggs in a bowl. Add spring onion, salt & pepper.

3. Heat butter in a skillet/pan. Pour the egg mixture and roll the pan to spread the egg evenly. Sprinkle chicken & tomatoes immediately.

4. Cook on low heat till set. Flip the omelette and cook the other side for a few seconds. Serve folded.

Banana French Toast

Brown sugar and cinnamon add loving warmth to these banana sandwiches that are dipped in egg then pan-fried till golden.

Makes 4

INGREDIENTS

2 eggs
1 ripe banana - mashed
2 tbsp brown sugar, or to taste
¼ tsp ground cinnamon (*dalchini powder*)
4 slices of bread
4 tbsp oil for shallow frying

METHOD

1 Whisk one egg in a broad, flat bowl. Keep aside.

2 Mash the banana in a small bowl. Add sugar and cinnamon powder to it.

3 Spread half of the mashed banana on a slice. Press another slice on it.

4 Dip the banana sandwich in the beaten egg. Turn after a minute so that the other side also gets coated with the egg.

5 Heat 2 tbsp oil on a non stick griddle/*tawa* or pan. Spread oil to cover the base of the pan.

6 Gently put the sandwich in the hot pan. Reduce heat and cook for a minute till the egg gets done. Turn to cook the other side too. Press lightly while cooking.

7 Remove from pan, cut into 2 pieces and serve warm. Repeat with the other slices.

Sunny Buns

Cooked carrots and peas are filled into hollowed-out buttered buns, topped with an egg, and sprinkled with cheese. When they are baked the egg sets beautifully in the middle.

Serves 4

INGREDIENTS

4 whole wheat burger buns
2 tbsp tomato ketchup
2 tbsp butter
4 eggs
½ onion - chopped (¼ cup)
1 carrot - chopped finely (½ cup)
2 tbsp peas
¼ tsp salt, ¼ tsp pepper, or to taste
4 tbsp grated cheddar cheese

GARNISH
red chilli flakes or freshly crushed peppercorns

METHOD

1. Slice the top of each bun and scoop out neatly to make a hollow bun, leaving ¼" wall all around.

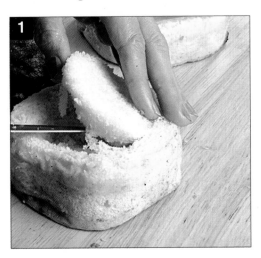

2. Spread some tomato ketchup in the hollow part of the buns. Butter the edges and the sides of the buns lightly. Keep aside.

3. Heat 1½ tbsp butter and saute onion till soft. Add the carrots and peas. Cook for 2-3 minutes. Remove from heat and add salt & pepper to taste.

4. Spoon the carrot-pea mixture in the hollow bun.

5. Break an egg on the vegetables in the bun. Repeat the same with the remaining buns.

6. Sprinkle cheese over the egg and bake all the buns in a pre-heated oven at 200°C/400°F for about 10 minutes till the white is set, the cheese gets melted and the buns are crisp.

7. Sprinkle red chilli flakes or black pepper. Serve hot.

Veggie Scrambled Eggs

Five vegetables – spinach, carrots, bell peppers, peas and tomatoes – are stirred into the eggs to make a complete meal.

Serves 2

INGREDIENTS

2 eggs
2 tsp butter
1 onion - chopped (½ cup)
3-4 leaves of spinach - shredded
2 tbsp finely chopped carrots
2 tbsp chopped green bell peppers
2 tbsp peas (boiled or frozen)
1 tomato - cut into 4 pieces, remove pulp and chop finely
2 tbsp milk
2 tbsp chopped cilantro/green coriander
salt and pepper to taste

METHOD

1 Beat eggs till fluffy. Keep aside.

2 Heat butter. Add onions and stir fry till onion turns soft.

3 Add spinach and carrots. Stir fry for a few minutes or till carrots are crisp tender.

4 Add bell peppers, peas and tomato. Stir to mix well.

5 Add whisked eggs and stir continously on medium heat till the egg scrambles.

6 Add milk, cilantro, salt & pepper. Serve with buttered toasts.

Freshly Baked Breads

& Grilled Bites

Herbed Bread Loaf

Learn how to make fresh-baked bread at home – this loaf is filled with herbs and topped with tomatoes and olives.

Serves 6

INGREDIENTS

250 g/8 oz whole wheat flour (*atta*)
½ tsp each of dried herbs - oregano,
dry parsley flakes, red chilli flakes
15 g/½ oz fresh yeast (2½ level tbsp)
or 1 tbsp dry yeast
1 tsp salt, 1 tbsp grain sugar
2 tbsp oil, ¼ cup milk
¾ cup warm water

TOPPING

1 tomato - cut into slices
a few black olives - sliced
2 tbsp chopped fresh parsley
salt and pepper to sprinkle
1 tsp poppy seeds (*khus khus*) to sprinkle

TOP GLAZE

1 egg white mixed with 1 tbsp water
or 2 tbsp full fat milk

METHOD

1 Put warm water in a bowl. Add sugar & yeast. Cover & keep aside for 15 minutes till frothy & it rises.

2 Sift flour in a big mixing bowl. Add all herbs. Add frothy yeast, salt and oil to flour. Mix it nicely. Add warm water gradually and knead with your palms till smooth and no longer sticky. Keep kneading with wet hands to get a soft and smooth dough.

3 To make it elastic put the dough on a lightly floured platform. Push the dough forward with your palms, fold over towards you with the fingers and push again with the palm. Give the dough a turn and knead again. Knead till very smooth for about 10-15 minutes. You can knead the dough in the food processor.

4 To check if it is done, roll it into a ball and stretch lightly. If it spreads roughly, knead for some more time to get a soft and smooth dough. (Do not over knead).

5 Put dough in a bowl. Cover with a cling film. Keep aside to prove for 1½-2 hours till double in size.

6 Punch dough lightly. Put it in a well greased loaf tin. Keep it aside undisturbed in a warm place to prove for about 30 minutes or till almost double in size.

7 Top with tomatoes, olives and parsley. Sprinkle some poppy seeds. Brush with egg white or milk. Bake in a preheated oven at 200°C/400°F for about 12-15 minutes, until light golden from the top.

Lemon Honey Chicken Sandwiches

Microwave the chicken for quick cooking; mix shredded chicken with honey and lemon; fill into sandwiches along with mayonnaise, cheese and veggies – when you grill them till golden they become irresistible.

Serves 2

INGREDIENTS

4 slices bread - lightly buttered
125 g/4 oz chicken, 1 tsp oil
1 tbsp lemon juice
1 tsp honey, 1 tsp mustard
salt and pepper to taste
2-3 lettuce leaves
4 tbsp mayonnaise
¼ cup shredded cabbage, ¼ cup corn
2 tbsp grated mozzarella cheese

METHOD

1 Prick chicken. Place chicken with lemon juice, oil and ¼ tsp salt in a dish. Mix. Cover with a plastic wrap and microwave for 3 minutes. Cool. Debone, cut into long strips. Mix chicken with honey. Add a pinch of pepper. Check taste. Add more honey and lemon juice if needed. Keep aside.

2 Add corn and shredded cabbage to mayonnaise and mix well. Check seasonings, add a pinch of pepper and salt if needed.

3 Lay a letuce leaf on a slice on the unbuttered side of the bread. Spread the mayonnaise mixture on the lettuce. Top with half of the lemon honey chicken. Sprinkle 1 tbsp grated mozzarella cheese. Cover with another slice, keeping the buttered side on the outside.

4 Repeat with the other two slices. To serve, put under a grill on the rack in the oven or heat on a grill pan till golden on both sides. Cut diagonally. Top with a small piece of lettuce and an olive pierced on a toothpick.

Variation: *Can use avocado instead of corn and cabbage. Cut avocado in half. Scoop out the pulp and chop finely.*

Freshly Baked Bread Wheels

Homemade bread! The dough is ready, roll them into wheels or make any shape you like.
To warm the bread, wrap in a cloth napkin and microwave for just 5-10 seconds.
Overheating will make them hard, leathery and chewy.

Makes 28 small ones

INGREDIENTS

250 g/8 oz whole wheat flour (*atta*)
2 tbsp fresh herbs (1 tbsp each of
chopped basil & coriander stalks)
¼ tsp each of dried herbs - oregano,
dry parsley flakes, red chilli flakes
15 gm fresh yeast (2½ tbsp)
1 tsp level salt
1 tbsp grain sugar
2 tbsp oil, ¼ cup milk
¾ cup warm water

FILLING (MIX TOGETHER)
¾-1 cup grated cheddar cheese
¼ tsp pepper
½ tsp red chilli powder
4-5 olives - thinly sliced

TOP GLAZE
1 egg white mixed with 1 tbsp water
or 2 tbsp full fat milk

METHOD

1 Put warm water in a bowl. Add sugar & yeast. Cover & keep aside for 15 minutes till frothy & it rises.

2 Sift flour in a big mixing bowl. Add fresh and dry herbs. Add frothy yeast, salt and oil to flour. Mix it nicely. Add warm water gradually and knead with your palms till smooth and no longer sticky. Keep kneading with wet hands to get a soft and smooth dough.

3 To make it elastic put the dough on a lightly floured platform. Push the dough forward with your palms, fold over towards you with the fingers and push again with the palm. Give the dough a turn and knead again. Knead till very smooth for about 10-15 minutes. You can knead the dough in the food processor too.

4 To check if it is done, roll it into a ball and stretch lightly. If it spreads roughly, knead for some more time to get a soft and smooth dough. (Do not over knead).

5 Put dough in a bowl. Cover with a cling film. Keep aside to prove for 1½-2 hours till double in size.

6 Mix all the ingredients of filling together. Keep filling aside.

7 Punch dough lightly. Divide the dough into 4 equal balls. Dust some flour on the platform. Roll out each ball into a thick tortilla/chappati of about 1/8" thickness.

8 Cut 1" from all the sides to get a rectangular shape. Spread some filling on the upper portion.

9 Fold the top part to cover the filling. Roll on till the end to get a roll. Dip the knife in flour to avoid sticking, cut the roll into 1" pieces.

10 Place the rolls with the cut side up, on a very well greased tray.

11 Keep it aside undisturbed in a warm place to prove for about 30 minutes or till almost double in size.

12 Brush with egg wash or milk. Bake in a preheated oven at 200°C/400°F for about 12-15 minutes, until light golden from the top.

Egg-Topped Toasts

More than just an egg sandwich – these terrific toasts have crunchy veggies and cheese to heighten your interest!

Makes 6

INGREDIENTS

6 slices bread - sides trimmed & toasted
till light brown
½ tomato- chopped finely
½ cup finely chopped green bell peppers
¼ tsp freshly crushed peppercorns
2 hard-boiled eggs
3-4 tbsp grated cheddar cheese
3 tbsp salsa, optional

SPREAD
3 tbsp butter
½ cup grated mozzarella cheese
¼ tsp mustard powder
¼ tsp pepper powder, ¼ tsp salt

METHOD

1 Separate the yolk and the white of the boiled eggs.

2 Mix all the ingredients of the spread in a bowl. Add the egg yolks. Mix till a smooth spread is ready. Check seasonings. Keep aside.

3 Spread the egg yolk mixture on the slices.

4 Chop the egg whites into tiny pieces. Mix bell peppers and tomato with it. Add salt to taste.

5 Top with chopped egg white and tomato mixture. Sprinkle some grated cheddar cheese. Sprinkle some freshly crushed peppercorns.

6 At the time of serving, keep the prepared slices in a preheated grill on a wire rack for 3-4 minutes.

7 Cut into two triangles if desired. Serve hot dotted with salsa.

Sesame Spinach Oat Toasts

Crunchy toasted oats combine with spinach and milk to make a wonderful spread – top with sesame seeds and create a sensation!

Serves 2

INGREDIENTS

½ cup oats
4 bread slices
1 cup finely chopped spinach leaves
1 small onion - chopped (½ cup)
1½ tbsp butter
salt, pepper to taste, ½ cup milk
4 tsp tomato ketchup
2 tsp sesame seeds (*til*)
a few tomato or red bell pepper strips

METHOD

1 Heat 1½ tbsp butter. Add oats, cook for 3-4 minutes on low heat.

2 Add the chopped onion. Saute for a minute.

3 Add the chopped spinach. Saute for 2 minutes. Add salt and pepper. Mix.

4 Add milk stirring continuously with the other hand. Cook for 1-2 minutes. Remove from heat. Keep aside.

5 Spread 1 tsp tomato ketchup on each slice.

6 Spread some oat-spinach mixture on it. Sprinkle sesame seeds.

7 Garnish with red strips.

8 Bake in a preheated oven at 200°C/ 400°F for 3-4 minutes or more till the bread gets toasted. Cut into 2 triangles or serve whole.

Jumbo Footlong

Tinned baked beans mixed with onions and bell peppers make an appetising filling – melting cheese on top is like the icing on the cake!

Serves 6

INGREDIENTS

1 French loaf or cheese loaf (any boat shaped loaf) - cut into two horizontally
2-3 tbsp butter - softened
(200 g/7 oz) tin baked beans (1¼ cups)
2 tbsp oil
2 onions - chopped finely (1 cup)
1 green bell pepper/capsicum - chopped finely (¾ cup)
a dash of tabasco, about ¼ tsp
salt, pepper - to taste
¼ cup grated cheddar cheese

METHOD

1   Slightly scoop out both the bread halves, leaving a border of 1" all around to from a boat. (The scooped out bread is not needed in this recipe, but add it to any croquette mixture to make them crisp.)

2   Soften butter and apply to the scooped out surface and the border of both the boats.

3   Heat oil in a pan and add onions and fry till soft.

4   Add bell peppers, stir for a minute. Add salt, pepper and tabasco. Remove from heat.

5   Add baked beans. Mix well. Pile this filling into the scooped out hollows of the French loaf.

6   Sprinkle grated cheese on the top. Grill for 3-4 minutes or microwave on medium power for 2 minutes till the cheese melts slightly. Serve hot.

Croquettes

& Sausages

Broccoli & Potato Rolls

Grated potatoes, broccoli and cheese are used to make these outstanding rolls – a crisp coating adds to the pleasure. Deep-fry or grill, as desired.

Makes 8

INGREDIENTS

1 small flower (250 g/8 oz) broccoli
375 g/12 oz (3-4) potatoes
2 tbsp milk, 1 tsp salt, ½ tsp pepper
1 cup grated mozzarella cheese
1 bread slice - grind in a mixer to get fresh crumbs (½ cup)

COATING

¼ cup flour (*maida*) mixed with ½ cup milk
1 cup fresh bread crumbs (from 2 slices) mixed with 1 tsp oregano and ¼ tsp salt

METHOD

1. To blanch broccoli, break into florets. Wash florets, put in a microproof dish. Sprinkle 2 tbsp water and microwave covered for 2 minutes. Remove from dish. Wash and put potatoes in the dish. Sprinkle 2 tbsp water. Microwave covered for 5 minutes or till soft.

2. Peel and grate potatoes from the fine side of the grater to get 2 cups grated potatoes. Add milk, salt & pepper. Beat well with a spoon till smooth and slightly fluffy.

3. Chop broccoli finely to get about 1 cup. Add broccoli and cheese to potatoes. Add fresh crumbs so that it is firm enough to be shaped into rolls. Check salt. Make 2" long, thick rolls. Flatten the sides.

4. Grind 2 slices of bread with salt and oregano to get 1 cup fresh crumbs. Dip rolls in a batter of flour and milk. Roll over seasoned bread crumbs.

5. Deep-fry 2-3 pieces at a time, on medium heat till golden brown. Alternately, sprinkle some oil on the rolls or spray with non stick spray and grill till golden, turning sides in between.

Tuna Croquettes

These delicate croquettes will thrill your taste buds – a tuna and corn filling wrapped in a thin lemon-flavoured crust – to die for!

Serves 2

INGREDIENTS

185 g/6 oz tuna (in brine)
1 tsp lemon juice, 2 tbsp corn
2 tbsp coriander or parsley - chopped
1 tsp tomato ketchup, salt & pepper to taste
oil for shallow frying

COATING

1 egg white mixed with 1 tbsp water
½ cup dry bread crumbs
1 tsp lemon rind/zest, optional

METHOD

1 Mix tuna with lemon juice. Add corn, chopped parsley, ketchup, a pinch of salt and pepper, or to taste.

2 Shape into small croquettes or rolls with flat edges.

3 Grate the outer yellow skin of the lemon to get rind. Mix it with dry bread crumbs. Beat the egg white with some water to make egg wash. Dip the croquettes in egg wash, roll over bread crumbs to coat.

4 Fry the croquettes in medium hot oil in a pan/skillet until golden, drain on a paper. Serve with ketchup and buttered toasts.

Sausage Stuffed Mushrooms

Mushrooms are marinated for added flavour, then stuffed with sausage, parsley and cheese and gently sautéed in butter – they will disappear off the plate in minutes!

Serves 4

INGREDIENTS

12 large mushrooms
2 tbsp balsamic vinegar
¼ tsp each - salt and pepper
4 cocktail sausages (chicken or pork)
2 tbsp butter
2 tbsp mozzarella cheese
1 tbsp chopped parsley or coriander

METHOD

1 Gently remove the stalk from the mushrooms. Keep aside.

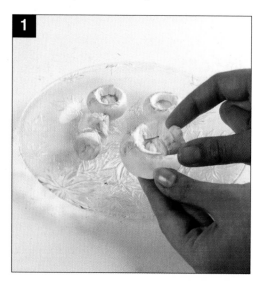

2 Chop the mushroom stalks finely. Marinate the mushroom heads in salt, pepper and balsamic vinegar.

3 Cut sausages into slices.

4 Heat 1 tbsp butter in a pan, add the mushroom stalks, stir fry till they change colour slightly.

5 Add the sausages, cook for 1-2 minutes, till the mixture turns dry. Sprinkle salt and pepper to taste. Remove from heat. Add cheese and parsley.

6 Stuff the mushroom cups tightly with the mixture.

7 Heat 1 tbsp butter in a pan. Place the stuffed mushrooms in the pan. Cover and cook for 2 minutes. Serve with any bread of your choice with the leftover filling on the side.

Breakfast Sausage Platter

The look is professional, but so easy to make – a platter of sautéed cabbage and apples, eggs and sausages.

Serves 2

INGREDIENTS

4-6 breakfast sausages (chicken or pork)
½ tsp oregano
2 tsp butter
2½ cups shredded cabbage
1 tsp Worcestershire sauce or any stir fry sauce
salt and pepper to taste
1 apple - cut into wedges
2 hard-boiled eggs - cut into round slices or wedges
a few sprigs of parsley

METHOD

1 Heat 1 tsp butter in pan. Add the cabbage, stir fry on high heat for ½ minute. Add the sauce, salt & pepper, remove on to the serving platter or a plate.

2 Put sausages in a non stick pan on low heat. Cook stirring continuously until well browned (sausages cook in their own fat, you may add 2-3 tbsp of water if the pan is not non stick). Sprinkle oregano on them. Mix and remove from pan.

3 In the same pan, saute apple pieces in 1 tsp butter and sprinkle a pinch of salt and pepper on them.

4 Arrange the cooked sausages on cabbage. Arrange apples and boiled eggs also on the sides. Heat in the microwave for just 1 minute. Garnish with parsley. Serve.

Jalapeno & Cheese Croquettes

When a feather-light filling like ricotta cheese is used, it needs to be handled with care - get the know-how in this easy-to-follow recipe and make perfect croquettes each time.

Serves 3-4

INGREDIENTS

125 g/4 oz ricotta cheese or grated *paneer*
1 cup grated mozzarella cheese
2-3 jalapenos - chopped finely (1 tbsp)
1 slice of bread
½ tsp black pepper powder
½ tsp salt, or to taste
oil for frying

TO COAT
½ cup plain flour (*maida*)
1 cup dry bread crumbs mixed with 1 tsp
mustard powder and ¼ tsp salt

METHOD

1 Tear a bread slice into pieces and grind in a mixer to get fresh crumbs.

2 Mix ricotta cheese/grated paneer, mozarella cheese, jalapenos, pepper, salt and fresh bread crumbs. Add more bread crumbs if the mixture is not firm enough to handle.

3 Divide the mixture into equal portions. Shape each into a roll, about 2" long. Flatten the sides of the roll, by pressing the sides of the roll against a flat surface. Keep aside.

4 Spread flour and bread crumbs in separate flat plates. Mix salt and mustard powder with bread crumbs. Take 1 cup of water separately in a shallow flat bowl. Roll a croquette over flour to coat. Now dip the croquette in water for a second and then immediately roll it over dry bread crumbs. All the sides should be completely covered with bread crumbs.

5 Heat oil in a pan/wok and fry 2 croquettes at a time till golden brown.

Pancakes

& Other Recipes

Breakfast Muffins

The muffin batter uses oil and milk and can be stirred up in a jiffy – a great treat for the family.

Makes 12

INGREDIENTS

220 g/7 oz flour
½ tsp salt, 1 tsp baking powder
2½ tbsp sugar
1 egg
60 ml/2 oz oil
220 ml/7 oz milk

TO SERVE
butter and jam

METHOD

1 Sift flour with salt and baking powder. Put in a mixing bowl. Add sugar and mix.

2 Beat egg lightly. Add oil and milk to the egg.

3 Stir the egg mixture into the flour, mixing just enough to moisten the flour and get a lumpy mixture. Do not mix too much.

4 Brush paper cups with oil. Arrange in a muffin pan.

5 Fill them with the muffin batter.

6 Bake in a preheated oven at 200°C/400°F for 20-25 minutes, till well risen and golden on the top.

7 Serve with butter and jam.

Mushroom-Topped Green Pancakes

Pureed spinach gives an intriguing green colour to the pancakes, and sautéed mushrooms give style and elegance.

Makes 15 small ones

INGREDIENTS

1 cup plain flour (*maida*)
1 egg
2 cups milk, approx.
2 cups finely chopped spinach leaves
2 pinches baking powder
¾ tsp salt, or to taste

TOPPING
2 tbsp oil
2 green onions chopped along with greens
or ¼ cup chopped regular onion
200 g/8 oz mushrooms - sliced thickly
1 tomato - cut into ½" pieces
salt and pepper to taste

METHOD

1. Cut the stems of the spinach and chop leaves finely. Blanch for 2 minutes in boiling water. Strain and squeeze excess water. This makes about ½ cup chopped and blanched leaves.

2. Mix flour, egg, milk, spinach, baking powder, salt and pepper well to get a thick pouring batter. Keep aside for 15 minutes.

3. To prepare the topping, heat oil in a non stick pan. Add spring onion and stir for ½ minute. Add mushrooms, stir for 2-3 minutes, add tomato, salt and pepper. Mix and remove from fire. (The salt is added at the end, if salt is added earlier, the mushrooms leave water). Keep topping aside.

4. To prepare pancakes, heat a non-stick skillet/pan. Coat pan with 1 tsp oil or use a non stick spray to grease the pan/skillet.

5. Keeping the heat on medium, drop about 2 tbsp of batter with a small laddle (*kadchi*). Gently spread to make a small thickish pancake (pancake should not be thin). Make 3-4 pancakes in a batch.

6. When the bottom get cooked, turn the pancakes to cook the other side. Remove on a serving dish.

7. Top the spinach pancakes with 1 heaped tbsp of hot mushroom topping. Serve hot.

Note: *Corn and tiny florets of broccoli can be substitued for mushrooms. Use ½ cup corn and 1 cup tiny florets of broccoli instead of mushrooms.*

Grilled Oat Potatoes

Who say potatoes are unhealthy & fattening! Yes, they are if you fry them. Here we have stuffed them with a delicious filling and grilled them to perfection.

Serves 4

INGREDIENTS

4 large potatoes
1 cup chopped ham or boiled chicken
2 tbsp peas - frozen or boiled
¼ cup oats
½ cup yogurt
2 tbsp grated carrots
½ tsp salt, ½ tsp black pepper
1 tbsp melted butter

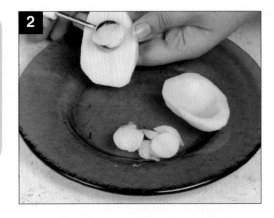

METHOD

1 Wash potatoes well. Put wet potatoes in a flat dish in a single layer and cover them. Microwave for 5 minutes. Check after 3-4 minutes to see if soft. Peel if you like.

2 Cut the boiled potato lengthwise. Scoop potato half with a melon baller, leaving ¼" wall all around.

3 Mix ham, peas, oats, yogurt and grated carrots. Add half of the scooped potato, salt & pepper. Check seasonings. Keep aside.

4 Brush the walls and the outside of the potatoes with melted butter.

5 Fill the mixture in the scooped potatoes, heaping them a little.

6 Place potato shells in a greased baking dish and bake at 180°C/ 350°F for 20 minutes. Serve hot dotted with tomato ketchup.

Indian Savoury Pancakes

These protein-rich pancakes are bursting with onions, tomatoes and peppers for maximum flavour.

Serves 2-3

INGREDIENTS

BATTER
¾ cup gram flour *(besan)*
¼ cup cornstarch
½ cup finely chopped onion
½ cup finely chopped tomato
1 green chilli/serrano pepper - seeded &
finely chopped, optional
1 tbsp chopped coriander leaves
½ tsp red chilli powder, ¾ tsp salt
½ tsp garam masala
1½ cups water, approx.

METHOD

1 Mix all ingredients of the batter together, except water.

2 Add enough water to the mixture to get a batter of a thick pouring consistency. Beat well.

3 Keep the batter aside for ½ hour.

4 Heat a non stick skillet/pan. Put 1 tbsp of oil on it and spread it on the base of the skillet. Alternately, use some non stick cooking spray.

5 Mix the batter well. Keeping the heat low, pour some batter on the skillet. Spread the batter a little with the back of the spoon, keeping it slightly thick.

6 After 2 minutes, pour 2 tsp of oil on the pancake. After the edges turn golden and the bottom is cooked, turn carefully.

7 Remove from skillet/pan after the other side also gets cooked and the onions turn a little brown.

8 Serve hot with mint chutney or tomato ketchup.

Pancake Sandwiches

Tablespoons of thin buttermilk batter are dropped on the hot pan to make small pancakes which are sandwiched with sweet, lemony ricotta – dreamily delicious!

Serves 2- 3

INGREDIENTS

¼ cup flour (*maida*)
½ tsp baking powder
1½ tbsp powdered sugar
1 egg - lightly beaten
¾ cup ready made buttermilk (*lassi*)

LEMON RICOTTA FILLING

½ cup ricotta cheese or home made *paneer*
2 tbsp lemon juice
2 tbsp powdered sugar
1 tbsp raisins

METHOD

1 Place flour, baking powder and sugar in a bowl and mix to combine. Make a well in centre of flour mixture, add egg and buttermilk and mix until smooth to get a thin pouring batter.

2 For the filling, mix ricotta cheese, lemon juice and sugar in a bowl. Keep aside.

3 Heat a nonstick frying pan over medium heat. Make small pancakes, each with 3 tbsp batter. Make as many as the pan can hold, leaving space between them. Drop tablespoons of batter into pan and cook for 1 minute each side or until golden. Remove pancakes, set aside and keep warm. Repeat with remaining batter to make more.

4 To assemble, take a pancake. Top with some ricotta filling and cover with another pancake. Make all sandwiches in the same way. Serve.

Corn Oat Upma

Powdered oats are cooked with corn, bell pepper and spices to produce a highly nutritious and satisfying dish. An all-time favourite!

Serves 2-3

INGREDIENTS

1 cup oats - powdered in a mixer
½ tsp mustard seeds (*sarson*)
1 dry, red chilli
10-12 curry leaves - optional
½ cup chopped onion
1 tomato - chopped
2 cups water
1½ tsp salt
½ cup corn kernels - boiled or frozen
½ bell pepper - chopped finely
juice of 1 lemon
4 tbsp oil

METHOD

1 In a clean heavy-bottomed pan, heat 4 tbsp oil. Reduce heat. Add mustard seeds. Add the dry red chilli and curry leaves.

2 Add onions. Fry till onions turn golden brown.

3 Add water and salt. Let it come to a boil.

4 Keeping the heat low, add chopped tomato and corn. Stir.

5 Add the powdered oats, gradually with one hand, stirring with the other hand continuously.

6 Stir fry for 3-4 minutes till dry. Turn off heat and add bell pepper and lemon juice. Mix well.

7 To serve, transfer some hot oat upma in a small bowl. Press lightly. Place the serving plate on the bowl and holding the bowl in one hand and pressing the plate with the other hand, invert the bowl on to the plate to get a heap for an individual serving.

GLOSSARY OF NAMES/TERMS

HINDI OR ENGLISH NAMES AS USED IN INDIA	ENGLISH NAMES AS USED IN USA/UK/ OTHER COUNTRIES
Basmati rice	Fragrant Indian rice
Capsicum	Bell peppers
Chaawal, Chawal	Rice
Choti Elaichi	Green cardamom
Chilli powder	Red chilli powder, Cayenne pepper
Cornflour	Cornstarch
Coriander, fresh	Cilantro
Cream	Whipping cream
Dalchini	Cinnamon
Degi Mirch	Paprika
Elaichi	Cardamom
Gajar	Carrots
Gobhi	Cauliflower
Hara Dhania	Cilantro/fresh or green coriander
Hari Mirch	Green hot peppers, green chillies, serrano peppers
Ham	Sliced, cooked pork meat
Jeera Powder	Ground cumin seeds
Kaju	Cashewnuts
Khumb	Mushrooms
Kishmish	Raisins
Maida	All purpose flour, Plain flour
Mitha soda	Baking soda
Paneer	Home made cheese made by curdling milk with vinegar or lemon juice. Fresh home made ricotta cheese can be substituted.
Panini	Toasted sandwiches made with Italian/Fresh bread
Pesto	Sauce of crushed basil leaves, pinenuts and olive oil
Pyaz, pyaaz	Onions
Red chilli flakes	Red pepper flakes
Saboot Kali mirch	Peppercorns
Saunf	Fennel
Salsa	A spicy tomato sauce of Mexican origin
Salami	Sliced Italian sausage
Slivered Almonds	Thinly sliced almonds
Soda bicarb	Baking soda
Spring Onions	Green onions, Scallions
Suji	Semolina
Til	Sesame seeds